Loren M. Powers

The Better Way

Hebrews
Study Guide
by
JACK CONN

BIBLE STUDIES
An Aldersgate Publication

New Horizons Study Books You Will Enjoy . . .

Origins of Life and Faith
(Genesis 1-28)

Trial and Triumph
(Genesis 29-50)

Crises at the Crossroads
(Ruth/Esther)

Songs of the Ages
(Psalms)

Herald of Hope
(Isaiah)

The Servant Story
(The Gospel of Mark)

That You May Believe
(John)

From Behind Closed Doors
(Acts 1-14)

To Rome and Beyond
(Acts 15-28)

Resources for Renewal
(Romans)

Under Construction
(Ephesians)

Open Letters from a Roman Prison
(Philippians/Colossians/Philemon)

The Better Way
(Hebrews)

At Ease Under Pressure
(James/I, II Peter)

The Power to Become
(I, II, III John/Jude)

The Victorious Christ
(Revelation)

Copyright 1985, Light and Life Press
Winona Lake, Indiana
Printed in U.S.A.

ISBN 0-89367-103-7

New Horizons Bible Studies, Undated material published for the Aldersgate Publications Association by Light and Life Press, 999 College Avenue, Winona Lake, Indiana 46590. Printed in U.S.A.

Contents

Editor: Jeff Hoyer

Adult Electives Committee: Jack Mottweiler, Dorothy Barratt, David Holdren, Stephen Miller, Carl Pierce, Gene Van Note, Lyle Williams

Editorial Board: Jack Mottweiler, Dorothy Barratt, Ronald Driggers, Douglas Feazell, David Holdren, Robert Kline, David Mann, Gene Van Note

To The Student

Welcome to the exciting world of NEW HORIZONS. You are on the threshold of discovery as you begin probing God's Word through the innovative design of this understandable Bible study series.

Personal study, Sunday school or small group study — no matter what shape the package, this Bible study is for you.

Before you turn to the next page, look over some pointers on how to get the most from this study.

Make Study a Habit. Set aside a specific time to enrich your life through a careful study of God's Word. If you are in a study group or just want added help, you will find the *New Horizons Leader's Guide* for this study unit a helpful book to have in addition to your study guide.

Keep a Diary. You will learn new things and gain exciting insights throughout this study. Record them. You will be glad you did. Your study notebook will become your own priceless treasure. "What will I keep in it?" you ask. Your diary is your own. It can be as basic or complicated as you make it. For starters, you might just want to record main insights you discover each time you study. If a more detailed diary appeals to you, include scriptural themes which occur throughout the study passages, insights about God, chapter summaries, answers to questions from the student book, and discoveries that have personal application in your life.

Advanced Study. If you're the kind of person who likes to dig in and go all out in deeper study, the *Optional Advanced Section* of each session will appeal to you. Although this section is not usually covered as part of the regular session, it provides an outlet for those who want a deeper study of each session. Dust off the Bible handbooks. Dig out the concordances and Bible dictionaries. You will want to use them to tackle the big questions under the *Optional Advanced Section.*

Technique. There is a big difference between reading your Bible and studying it. In life, anything worth doing is worth doing well. Bible study is no exception. Much of doing something well is knowing how to go about it. Here are a few techniques which are helpful in Bible study.

Color Coding. If you don't mind marking in your Bible, you can use colored pencils and color code various passages. Different colors

4

existence. One of the real dangers addressed in the epistle is that of going back to the old ways and denying Christ as the fulfillment of the sacrificial system once and for all.

The epistle to the Hebrews can be divided into two main divisions. In the first division the writer sets forth a doctrinal exposition (1:1 — 10:18). It is God's full and final revelation of himself to man in the person of His Son, Jesus Christ. The second division (10:19 — 13:25) is practical. It reveals how the life made possible by knowing Jesus better as our High Priest within the Holy Place is now our high privilege. The Son of God has opened the Holy of Holies in heaven. Anchor your hope there in Him and the heavenly life can be experienced as He imparts it. We need to know the great doctrinal truths of holiness and to experience them. It is by knowledge and experience that we gain stability and growth in the Christian life.

1 A Manner of Speaking

Read Hebrews 1

How do you communicate truth to someone who has been exposed to lies?

You begin by focusing on common ground, something you both agree on, then you move to points of controversy.

The letter to the Hebrews begins by focusing on God. There are no gods, only one God. The Hebrews knew and believed this truth. The writer then moves beyond barriers to show the superiority of God's complete and final revelation in Christ.

As you study Hebrews 1 notice how the author carefully and logically provides proof of Christ as God's perfect revelation of himself.

GOD SPEAKS. 1:1-3

In the past God spoke in a manner which Hebrew readers understood and were proud of. God singled out the Hebrew nation and spoke to their fathers through His prophets. They had a rich heritage. They were a chosen people. They had traditions. In these last days, they were favored again. God chose to send His Son as a full revelation of himself, and His Son was born a Jew.

1. Why do you think the writer of Hebrews began his letter by emphasizing "God spoke"? To whom and through whom did God speak (v. 1)? What might be examples of "times" and "ways" in which He spoke?

2. Hebrews is addressed to believers in one God. If you are a Christian, how would you start to explain Jesus to an unbeliever or someone who believed in many gods? If you are not yet a believer, describe the type of approach to which you would respond the most favorably.

3. The word "but" (v. 2) sets up a contrast between verses 1 and 2. Describe and compare what is contrasted.

The writer of Hebrews knew that those he addressed had to know the special place the Son occupied if they were to have a saving faith and experience His presence in their hearts. The basis of Christianity is the fact that Jesus is the eternal Son of God made flesh through a miracle of virgin birth.

4. According to verse 2, what is special about the Son? Why is it important that Jesus be recognized as the Son of God rather than just a prophet or great teacher?

5. What does the word "heir" reveal about the relationship between God and the Son?

6. Since the Son is revealed as God's agent in creation (v. 2) what does this suggest about your responsibility, as a created being, to Him?

7. Describe who the Son is and what He does (v. 3). What does it mean to you personally to know He is not only the "Creator" but also the "Sustainer"?

8. Describe what you think is meant by the phrases "radiance of God's glory" and "exact representation of his being."

9. What was the Son's role in God's plan to save you according to verse 3b?

The words "sat down" (v. 3) implies that Christ completed His mission. The phrase "right hand of the Majesty" suggests the Father's approval and acceptance.

10. In what ways do we depend on the Son to know the Father, and on the Father to know the Son?

BETTER THAN ANGELS. 1:4-14

The writer of Hebrews declares the Son is superior to (better than) the angels. The Greek word *Kreisson* is the comparative degree of a word meaning "strong" or "powerful" in activity or effect. It is translated in the *King James Version* as "better." The word is used twelve times in the letter. There is often no better way of knowing or understanding something than by placing it in contrast with what is less perfect.

The writer also quotes from II Samuel, Deuteronomy, and Psalms to lift up Christ as the Son of God. He uses contrasts to show that although angels are good and the past communications from God were good, Christ is "better." The writer of Hebrews does not pressure his readers, he leads them.

11. According to verse 4 what has Christ inherited? What does this imply about the relationship between God and Christ?
12. What "proof" is given in verse 5 of Christ's superiority over the angels? What command of God's is given in verse 6? In what way does this command imply Christ's superior position?
13. What does verse 7 reveal about angels? Compare verse 7 with verse 14.

"His angels winds," and his servants "flames of fire" (v. 7) refer to the function and position of angels as servants of God.

14. What do verses 8-12 reveal about the Son? What is revealed about angels in constrast to Christ in verses 13-14?

From a historical perspective, angels had often communicated God's will to the Jewish people. Angels were seen as mediators between God and man. It is easy to see how some persons may have been tempted to have an almost superstitious regard for them and in some cases even worship them. Such a temptation was real to the Hebrews and the writer of the letter in this first chapter quickly places these heavenly beings in their proper place.

15. Have you ever been tempted to follow a messenger (Christian friend, pastor) of God rather than the Son of God? Explain. In what ways might it be easy to fall prey to such a temptation? Why is it wrong?

INSIGHT/ACTION

16. God chose to speak to mankind in two stages — the Old Testament and through His Son. Why do you think He revealed himself in this way?
17. Summarize briefly the main emphasis covered in Hebrews chapter 1 and describe why the emphasis is important for the believer today.

OPTIONAL ADVANCED STUDY

18. Use an appropriate study Bible or Bible handbook to identify the Old Testament quotes contained in Hebrews 1. Describe in your study diary the importance of these quotes as they relate to the topics contained in Hebrews chapter 1.

2 Red Flags and Open Ears

Read Hebrews 2

Poison. Keep out of the reach of children! ("You are free to eat from any tree in the garden; but you must not eat from the tree of the knowledge of good and evil . . ." Genesis 2:16-17a.)

Warning! Shoplifters will be prosecuted! ("You shall not steal" Exodus 20:15.)

These previous warnings reveal that situations may change but mankind remains the same. The admonitions of the past seem strangely similar to the present.

Warnings usually imply that there is a penalty to be imposed if the warning is disregarded. The penalty may not be immediate but it will come.

In Hebrews chapter 2, the author of the letter gives the first of five warnings which appear in his letter. As you read the writer's spiritual warning you will realize it is relevant today.

STOP, LOOK, AND LISTEN. 2:1-4

The Bible begins in Genesis with a warning to the first couple and ends in Revelation with a warning for all persons. The writer to the Hebrews reminded the believers to keep in clear perspective the basis for their belief.

1. To what does the word "therefore" refer (v. l)? What does the writer tell the Hebrews to do? Why? Describe why following his advice would encourage spiritual growth. Is the advice practical today? Explain.

2. What are examples of things that might cause one to drift away from spiritual truth? How could being a good listener spiritually help you resist such influences?

3. When was the last time you felt that you had spiritual guidance? Where and how did you receive it? In what ways did it involve other people?

A very significant Greek word in verse 1 is translated in the *King James Version* (slip). A more accurate translation of the word is "drift"

(NIV). In verse 1 the word implies flowing or passing by without giving due heed. Drifting contains the idea of moving slowly a little at a time from a higher level to a lower level. Drifting requires no sense of direction or goal. A person who drifts loses awareness of his location. No reference points are maintained. The drifter can be in danger without realizing it. We must be aware of the direction of growth in our Christian walk — are we growing closer to God or further from Him.

4. Is "drifting" restricted to individuals or is it possible for a church, city, or nation to drift? Explain.

5. Is having a Christian heritage a help or hinderance in avoiding spiritual drifting?

Verses 2-4 highlight the basis of responsibility. The Hebrews' position of greater privilege (having experienced salvation) placed them in a position of greater responsibility. The Hebrews had no excuse for disobedience and neither do we.

6. Describe in your own words what you think the writer says in verses 2-3. According to verse 3 who first announced this salvation and who confirmed it?

7. In what specific ways did God add His authority to the confirmation of salvation (v. 4)? Describe in your own words what is meant by the term "salvation."

HUMBLED, HURT, AND HONORED. 2:5-10

In verses 5-10 the writer to the Hebrews begins to explain the mystery of God's dealing with humanity.

8. What is revealed about angels and their position according to verse 5?

9. Describe what you think the relationship is between angels and humanity today.

10. Describe in your own words what you think is meant by verse 8. In what way was Jesus "made a little lower than the angels" (v. 9)?

11. According to verse 9 how is Jesus now crowned? Why? What does His death mean for all persons? What does it mean to you?

12. How was Christ "perfected" (v. 10)? To whom do you owe your existence? What does your life reveal about how you feel about your responsibility to God (personal)?

OUR BROTHER, THE KING. 2:11-13

Jesus is holy. He is the one who made it possible for us to be holy by filling us with His Holy Spirit. He is the Creator and we are the created. He came from God in eternity. We came from His creation in time. We are sons of God as we partake of the divine life in Him. His sonship is original; ours is derived. But both are one because both originated in God. It is this oneness that is unique. It made it possible for Him to become one of us in our humanity and to impart to us that holiness we need. We are one family — the family of God.

13. What is it that the redeemed have that makes it possible for Jesus to call them "brothers" (v. 11)? How do the three passages from the Old Testament contained in verses 12-13 support or prove that Jesus and His believers are brothers?
14. Describe what you think the word "holy" (v. 11) means.

FREE AT LAST. 2:14-18

15. According to verses 14-15 what did Christ do? Why? What do you think is included in the term "death"? What does verse 15 imply about those who are willing to trust in Christ?
16. According to verse 16 who does Christ help? What do verses 17-18 reveal about Christ's purpose in becoming a man?
17. In the New Testament Jesus is called "High Priest" only in the letter to the Hebrews (v. 17). Explain what you think it means for Christ to be our "High Priest."
18. In what ways should verse 18 be an encouragement for anyone who is tempted?

INSIGHT/ACTION

19. What does Hebrews chapter 2 reveal about Christ and His relationship to humanity? Based on chapter 2, what help is available to you for living a successful Christian life?
20. Hebrews chapter 2 reveals what Christ was willing to do for you. Evaluate your own life and describe briefly what you are willing to do for Him.

OPTIONAL ADVANCED STUDY

21. Use Bible dictionaries and concordances to study the meaning of the following words: incarnation; salvation; atonement; and holiness. Record your insights in your study diary.

3 The Servant and the Son

Read Hebrews 3

There is a big difference between a servant and a son.

In Hebrews chapter 4 we see the contrast in detail. Moses is revealed as the servant of God who testified to what would be said in the future. Moses was good and faithful. He was revered by all Hebrews. But, Christ is "better." He is faithful as a son over God's house which is the community of believers.

Christ must have the center place in our worship. He is the spiritual bridge builder between God and humanity. He is not only the Creator, but also the Sustainer.

As we experience the "living" way He purchased, we know Him and come to know God.

THEREFORE BROTHERS . . . 3:1

1. What do you think is the central idea of verse 1?
2. To what do you think the word "therefore" (NIV) or "wherefore" (KJV) refers?
3. What term(s) does the writer use to address his readers? What do you think the term means? Define "apostle" and "high priest." In what ways are these terms appropriate descriptions of Christ?

The word "fix" (NIV) or "consider" (KJV) is said to be from the root of a Latin word for "star" and originally meant to "contemplate" the stars. It suggests the idea of one who quietly and patiently maintains a concentrated gaze on the heavenly bodies. Such a person seeks to know all he can about them. We are urged to fix our gaze on Jesus in like manner, to learn of Him.

4. Describe what you think it means to "share in the heavenly calling." Why is it spiritually dangerous to "fix" your thoughts on anything or anyone other than Christ?
5. What does it mean to "confess" Christ? What relationship is there between faith or believing and confessing Christ?

THE DIVINE CARPENTER. 3:2-6

Jesus was by trade a carpenter from Nazareth. He did not have the earthly credentials that the ruling church leaders felt were essential to even speak of religious things. However, in reality He was more than a lowly carpenter, He was the divine builder. By Him and through Him all things exist. He was faithful even to death to provide a sacrifice for our sin.

6. Describe what you think are basic qualifications for being chosen of God to be a spiritual leader. What were Moses' qualifications (vv. 2, 5)?
7. What does the phrase ''in all God's house'' (NIV) or ''in all his house'' (KJV) mean (v. 2)? Define ''faithful.''
8. Describe what you think the writer means in verse 3. What is the difference between a servant (v. 5) and a son (v. 6)?
9. How do ''we hold on to our courage and the hope of which we boast'' (v. 6)? What is implied by the word ''if''? In what ways is Christ a source of courage and hope?

APPEALING TO THE PAST. 3:7-11

This passage is cited from Psalm 95:7-11. It surely reminded the Hebrew readers of one of Israel's saddest periods — that of the wilderness wanderings. We should learn from past mistakes. The writer of the letter now begins to set the stage for his second warning by this appeal to the past.

10. Who is speaking and to whom does He speak (v. 7)? When does He speak? Do we have a choice in listening and hearing?
11. Define ''a hard heart.'' What can we do to keep a tender heart?
12. What penalty did God impose on the ''generation'' that hardened their hearts (v. 11)? God is love. How do you explain His wrath described in verses 7-11?

THE SECOND FLAG. 3:12-15

Unbelief has been and is the cause of all falling away from God. When faith slips away the unbelieving heart returns to its evil ways. Unbelief is the barrier that prevents the born again from going on into the enjoyment of Christ's promise and rest.

13. What warning is given in verse 12? How would you define a "sinful, unbelieving heart"?
14. Describe what meaning is carried by the expression "living God." Contrast and compare the worship of God with worship of idols.
15. What is the meaning of the saying "practice the presence of God"?
16. What can we do to develop our own faith and the faith of others (v. 13)? How often should we provide encouragement? Why?
17. Describe in your own words the conditional promise given in verses 14-15.

NO RESTING PLACE. 3:16-19

We need rest physically, emotionally, and mentally. Rest of the soul is also one of our longings.

Failure to find such rest cannot be placed upon God. Faith is the key to rest, and unbelief assures lack of rest. The early Hebrews longed for rest but lack of faith, lack of perseverance, stagnated progress, and deafness to the voice of God took its toll. We can learn from their negative example and not make the same mistake.

18. In one word, what caused the downfall of the persons described in verses 16-19? Did they have any valid excuse for their failure? Explain.
19. How does unbelief affect God? How does it affect humanity? Think of times in your own life when you have struggled with "belief." How did it affect you? What do verses 16-19 imply about belief?

INSIGHT/ACTION

20. Summarize briefly what Hebrews 3 teaches you about Jesus; His help in living Christlike lives; the importance of belief; and the need to encourage others in their faith.
21. List in your study diary specific things you have learned from Hebrews 3 that will help you grow spiritually.

OPTIONAL ADVANCED STUDY

22. Use Bible references to study the importance and meaning of faith. Record your insights in your study diary.
23. Search your Bible for examples of persons who trifled with faith (Samson, Solomon, Saul, Judas, Peter). List the things that caused their defeat in specific instances. Then, list positive things you can do to guard against the erosion of your faith.

4 In Search of Rest

Read Hebrews 4

Rest has always been important. It was especially meaningful to the Hebrews. Their greeting was not, "Hello, how are you?" It was, and still is, "Peace." The best blessing one Hebrew could bestow on another was carried in the greeting that is translated "Peace be to you," or "Let there be peace on your house." Other people of that time had no such greetings. For the Greeks it was "Joy." To the Romans it was "Health."

Why was the concept of "peace" or "rest" so important to the Hebrews? It was a result of their wilderness heritage. They came out of Egypt with a leader, Moses, who was helped by God's power. Ahead lay Canaan, the Promised Land. Yet, the Hebrews refused to enter because of unbelief. As a result there was no rest, only restless wandering. When at last the next believing generation exercised their faith, God settled them in Canaan. Therefore, there was no greater concept of blessedness to the Hebrew than to have peace — to be at rest.

In Hebrews 4, the writer to the Hebrews picks up the concept, "When you have started, Christian believer, do not rest until you are within the rest of God."

God's promise is still the same for all believers — come out of the bondage of sin and enter into the rest of a fully consecrated and sanctified life with Him.

LOOKING WITHIN. 4:1-3

The gospel of rest is preached in this passage to the Hebrew Christians as much as it was heralded by Moses, Caleb, or Joshua. Furthermore, it is to be a central message for believers today.

The element of warning in these verses is the same as the previous ones. Faith in God is a must. The early Hebrews failed and died short of the promised rest because of their unbelief. The lesson from the past is obvious. The time for faith to possess God's promise is now.

Moses delivered the children of Israel from Egypt; Joshua brought them into the rest of Canaan. We are brought out of sin by faith in Christ's redeeming work on the cross — it is there He redeemed and delivered us from bondage. We are brought into the rest of heaven by His ministry as the High Priest in the Holy of Holies. He is our Joshua — the one who brings us into His rest.

1. To what does "therefore" refer (v. l)? What still stands? What caution does the writer give? In what ways can a believer "fall short" of God's promise of rest? Why do you think the writer used the word "us" and then switched to the word "you" in the rest of his statement in verse 1?

2. What warning is implied in verse 2? How must the hearing of the things of God be treated if the message is to produce the intended effect?

3. What is the key to finding God's promised rest (v. 3)? Based on verse 3b describe what you think is meant by "rest" in this verse.

GOD AT REST. 4:4

God is a Spirit. Can a spirit become tired and require rest? One commentator explains the reference to rest in this verse by noting the Rabbi's conceptions which lie hidden behind the argument in this verse and surrounding verses.

God's rest was on the seventh day. According to Genesis 1 and 2 each of the first six created days had a "morning" and "evening" — a beginning and end. However, God's rest (the seventh day) contains no mention of an evening. Therefore, the Rabbis deducted that although the first six created days had a beginning and end, God's rest day was without end — an eternal rest.

God's eternal rest remains. It is available for all who will by faith believe and find rest in Him.

4. God's completed work of creation included the earth, our solar system, and the universe in which there is constant movement and change. Yet, He is immovable and changeless. What insight does verse 4 imply about God's rest even though there is constant activity and change in life?

5. Describe ways in which a believer can cultivate in his own life a holy stillness which is characteristic of God's presence, and is relatively uninfluenced by "things of life."

6. Describe the characteristics of a person (spiritual composure and life-style) who yields all to the Spirit of God and is a partaker of His rest.

RESTING IN THE ETERNAL. 4:5-8

7. Based on verses 5-6 why did some fail to find promised rest? Was the rest God spoke of limited to a time period? Explain. What do verses 7-8 reveal about the availability of such rest?

8. Describe what you think is meant by "today" in this passage. Why is it important to respond to God's offer today? Is the caution given in verse 7 relevant today? Explain.

TRUE REST. 4:9-11

There is a Sabbath rest reserved for the people of God. It is spoken of as a "remaining" in reference to Joshua and the rest of Canaan, which served as a type (example referring to something greater in the future) of the true rest that was to come. The true rest was made available through Christ. In Him we can now find perfect peace and eternal rest. It is not our works but His love that makes the difference. To rest in God is to yield one's being to the influence of a higher one for the continuation of a higher activity.

9. What does the word "remains" indicate about the availability of rest in God (v. 9)? Is such rest conditional? Explain.

10. What is implied in verses 10-11 about the believer's need to "rest in God" to live a successful Christlike life?

11. There were two stages in God's relation to His work — creation and then rest. Can you relate parallels to these in the Christian experience? Explain.

12. In what way can you rest in God and cease from works? Although it seems like a paradox, why is it necessary to "rest in God" rather than depend on works to get to heaven?

THE WORD AND THE EYES. 4:12-13

Of all the books that have been written, none have endured like the Bible. It is more than a book, it is the Word of God. It speaks to all humanity because the author is the Creator. His Word is living, active, and sharp.

13. In what ways is the Word of God (v. 12) "living" (NIV) or "quick" (KJV)? Have you ever felt the touch of the "living" Word? Explain. Have you seen it touch others? If so, what was the response?

14. In what ways is the Word of God "active" (NIV) or "powerful" (KJV)? What do you think the phrase "sharper than a double-edged sword" means? Paraphrase verse 12 in your own words.
15. What does verse 13 reveal about God? What does this verse reveal about each of us?

MEET YOUR HIGH PRIEST. 4:14-16

The high priest was a central figure in Old Testament worship of God. He was a mediator between God and the worshiper.

16. Who is the high priest referred to in verse 14? What are we told to do in verse 14 and why?
17. What does verse 15 reveal about Christ? Explain what the word "sympathize" means. Why is it a comfort to know Christ understands and sympathizes with us?
18. How should we approach the throne of grace (v. 16)? What is the reason we can take such an approach (v. 15)? Describe what you think is meant by "throne of grace."
19. What can we find at the throne of grace (v. 16)? What does this promise mean to you personally?

INSIGHT/ACTION

20. Summarize in one sentence the main focus of Hebrews 4.
21. Evaluate your own life. Have you found complete rest in God? If not, why not? Identify specific areas in your life that need to be more completely turned over to Him. Then, give Him complete control of your life if you have not already done so.

OPTIONAL ADVANCED STUDY

22. Look up the uses of "rest" as a noun in a Bible concordance. They will describe a state or place of relationship with God. List these words in your study diary. Also include brief descriptions of words of encouragement and promises God gives to all who seek to enter His rest.
23. Memorize Hebrews 4:12-13.

5 Greatness

Read Hebrews 5

"Great" and "greatest" are common words in today's vocabulary. TV commercials blare out that their drinks may be low in calories but they still have the "great" taste. Various performing acts claim to be "the greatest show on earth." All to often the "great" things of today are merely temporary entertainment that passes by without changing the lives it touches.

However, there is one greatness that is changeless, yet changes all it touches. That greatness can be found in Jesus Christ. He is great in who He is, how He lived, what He did and is doing for us as our High Priest in heaven. When by faith we understand and accept Him, we experience His greatness personally.

The writer to the Hebrews knew that his readers held their past leaders in great esteem. Their current high priest at the Temple held a special importance in the religious life of the nation as did the memory of the great line of high priests including the first, Aaron.

Although the early leaders were great the Hebrews needed to recognize Christ as the "greatest."

Hebrews chapter 5 confronts the danger among the early believers to make the revered leaders the focal point of faith. Such danger still exists today. Even though we do not see Christ with our physical sight He should still be the focus of our adoration, worship and faith. He is alive and He is the "greatest."

FEELING THE FEELINGS. 5:1-3

High priests were selected for a specific task. They were to serve at the altar and represent the nation of Israel in worship before God. The first 3 verses of chapter 5 highlight the characteristics required of earthly high priests that also can be found in perfect fulfillment in Jesus, our heavenly High Priest. The verses also note the weaknesses of the earthly high priests not to be found in Christ who was sinless.

1. According to verse 1 from among whom was the high priest chosen? What job did he have? Describe what offering "gifts and sacrifices for sin" involved. What is the difference between "selected" and "appointed?"

2. What emotions and feelings are implied in verse 2? Compare and contrast verse 2 with the description of Jesus, our perfect High Priest given earlier in 4:14-15. In what ways is it a comfort to know Christ understands our weaknesses?

3. What weakness of the earthly high priests is pointed out in verse 3? In what way is Christ, our High Priest different? Describe how you feel about Christ representing you before God.

CALLED TO GREATNESS. 5:4-6

A requirement for the high priest was that he be called by or have his appointment from God. Ideally it was not a matter of a priest deciding he wanted to be high priest and then by scheming and political maneuvering achieving the office.

It is against God that we have sinned. He has devised and implemented a way for us to find restored fellowship with Him. He has taken the initiative. It is God who we need and cannot find within ourselves or our own works; it is through Him and His love that we find a way opened. God provided the perfect High Priest, His own Son, to provide a way for us to find restored fellowship with Him. Christ did not take the position of High Priest by an elective process or self-appointment — God called Him.

4. What qualified Aaron to be the first high priest for the nation of Israel (v. 4)? In what ways is Christ a High Priest? What do verses 4-6 reveal about Christ?

The reference to Christ as a priest forever "in the order of Melchizedek" (v. 6) is mentioned as a point of comparison to imply the everlasting nature of His priesthood. Melchizedek is introduced in Genesis 14:18-20 as the mysterious king/priest of Salem to whom Abraham gave a tenth of his possessions. He lacked any named ancestors or descendants. His name means "king of righteousness." Also, Salem means peace. As the king of peace this mysterious Old Testament figure is seen to represent Christ who would be the perfect High Priest. He is referred to in greater detail in Hebrews chapter 7.

GREATNESS AND OBEDIENCE. 5:7-10

In verses 7-10 the writer refers to Jesus' prayer experience in Gethsemane the night of His betrayal. All of the Gospel writers describe the experience and here the writer to the Hebrews gives an independent witness to Christ's passion. The account gives a hint as to the widespread and familiar knowledge of the extent of the Lord's suffering that existed in the churches at the time. It reveals the importance placed upon that suffering experience.

Although Christ was the Son of God, He was also the Son of Man and suffered as one of us. He left us an example of submissiveness to God to follow.

The Gethsemane experience further qualified Christ to be our High Priest. He knows how we feel in life's experiences. He knows about pain and aloneness.

5. According to verse 7 what did Christ do while on earth? To what do you think "death" refers in verse 7? Since we know Christ went on to face physical death on the cross, what might the "heard" in verse 7 mean?

Some commentators believe that Christ (verse 7) was not seeking deliverance from death on the cross, but His soul dreaded the spiritual separation of that death — the identification with sin and the separation He would feel from God when God hid His face from Him. In a true sense, for a time Christ would feel the agony of a soul lost.

6. Describe the relationship between submission to God's will and expecting Him to hear and answer our prayers.
7. What did Christ learn from His suffering (v. 8)? How could He learn obedience when He had never disobeyed? What do you think is meant by "made perfect" (v. 9)? What happened as a result of His being made perfect? How has this affected you personally?
8. What part do you think obedience plays in finding new life in Christ? Is repentance a return to obedience? Explain. According to verse 9, what must each of us do to experience eternal salvation in and through Christ?

THE THIRD FLAG. 5:11-14

The third of five warnings in the letter begins here and continues into chapter 6.

The first warning was against indifference and neglect in the Christian life. The second was against unbelief and disobedience, and the third warning dealt with sloth and lack of progress in the Christian life.

Now the writer tries to arouse the Hebrew believers to the challenge of growth in the spiritual life. Those who have experienced spiritual birth must grow.

9. Why is it hard to explain deep spiritual truths to those who are slow to learn (v. 11)? What might be examples of things that cause slow spiritual learning?
10. What are some ingredients that you believe are basic to spiritual growth? In what way is sound doctrine or spiritual truth a basic need for spiritual growth?
11. What are examples of spiritual "milk" (v. 12)? What are examples of spiritual "solid food"?
12. According to verses 13-14 what are some evidences of spiritual maturity? Although Christ offers deliverance, what part do we play in our own salvation?

INSIGHT/ACTION

13. Describe in your own words the two main themes that appear in Hebrews chapter 5.
14. What does it mean to you personally to know that Christ is your High Priest before God? What are some things you can and should do to grow spiritually?

OPTIONAL ADVANCED STUDY

15. Use Bible reference material to study the duties and importance of the High Priest in the Old Testament setting. Compare and contrast these with Jesus in the role of High Priest.
16. Memorize Hebrews 5:8-10.

6 Good Traveling Company

Read Hebrews 6

The Christian life is a journey. It has movement and progress. The life begun at conversion must grow and mature.

Such spiritual growth manifests itself in many ways. Along with growth there will be the exercise of virtues, gifts, and works that surface when one becomes spiritually sensitive.

Hebrews chapter 6 concludes a warning against lack of progress in the Christian life. As you study the chapter you will realize spiritual growth is not only desirable for the believer, but it is an absolute necessity.

BEYOND THE BASICS. 6:1-3

Elementary teachings about Christ are essential. However, to remain spiritually healthy the believer must move forward to maturity and additional spiritual discovery.

1. According to verse 1, what is the believer to do? Define maturity. How does your definition compare with the word "perfection" (KJV)?
2. What do you think is meant by "elementary teachings about Christ"? Can these be discarded? Why or why not? What do you think is implied in "leaving the elementary teachings"?
3. What three pairs of elementary truths or doctrines are listed in verses 2-3?

As you study the three pairs of elementary teachings, note the first pair deals with the beginnings of Christian faith; the second pair deals with public confession of faith and church affiliation; and the third pair of truths relates to the future life. Each of the truths must be learned and are necessary for spiritual advancement. However, once obtained they must be maintained, not repeated over and over if growth in spiritual knowledge is to follow.

4. How would you describe "spiritual growth"? Is such growth internal, external or both? Explain.

5. As things grow they often change. In a spiritual sense does this give allowance for a believer to change some convictions as he/she grows spiritually? Explain.
6. What does verse 3 reveal about how the writer feels about spiritual growth?

IF THEY FALL AWAY. 6:4-8

7. Several statements are tied to the words "who have" in verses 4-5. List the statements. What do these phrases suggest about the spiritual experience of the person involved? What do you think it means to be "enlightened"?
8. What do you think is meant by "fall away" (v. 6)? What do verses 4-6 reveal about a person who falls away? Why will such a person reap the reward suggested?
9. In what ways is Christ "crucified" and "subject to public disgrace" by "believers" who forsake Him?
10. In what way is the illustration in verses 7-8 a good one to graphically illustrate the truths in verses 4-6?

In verse 6 the Greek word translated "to fall away" is *parapipto* which means to "fall in one's way." It signifies to fall away from an adherence to the realities and facts of the faith.

Some persons suggest that if a Christian falls he/she goes all the way to the bottom and must start over again. Such a position views Christians as cliff dwellers. In reality, an error recognized and confessed does not eliminate the foundation of faith — the believer can arise and go on.

Some persons do fall to irrecoverable depths. Such a danger is real. The writer to the Hebrews gives clear warning of such danger. God will not be mocked. A person who has known God and continues in his rejection of Him will reap the reward. It is serious business to trifle with faith and fail to press on to perfection (KJV) or maturity as set forth in the Word of God.

11. God is love and He is everywhere. Does universal love imply universal salvation? Is God's love the only factor in man's salvation? Explain.

HANG IN THERE. 6:9-12

"Beloved" (KJV) or "dear friends" (NIV) in verse 9 is not used anywhere else by the author in the book of Hebrews. It reveals his feeling towards his readers.

Often in churches there are believers who exist at varying levels of spiritual maturity. Usually there is a group composed of those who give themselves wholly to God — ever pressing onward to new spiritual ground as the Holy Spirit leads. Also present is a larger group composed of those who are content with a nominal possession of grace. Hebrews is addressed to both types of believers. In the warnings it speaks to both as if all were in danger. In the exhortations, encouragements, and words of commendation it speaks as if all shared the sentiments of those who were spiritual achievers. The writer tactfully did not pick on specific persons and cause barriers to arise. Alienated people neither hear nor respond, no matter how sound the doctrine may be.

12. What does the expression "dear friends" or "beloved" (KJV) reveal about the writer's attitude (v. 9)?
13. What might the advantages be in tempering warnings and stern truth with expressions of confidence and love?
14. What does verse 10 reveal about the audience to whom the writer spoke? What does verse 10 reveal about God? To whom is verse 11 addressed? What is the "hope" referred to in verse 11?
15. What simple and direct warning is given in verse 12? When is it good to imitate someone? According to verse 12, what two things are necessary to receive the promised inheritance?

PATIENCE AND THE PROMISE. 6:13-15

The Bible confirms that in the first Christian churches there were those who began well but failed to progress, then turned back. It still happens today. We can have God's promise only if we are diligent and persevere. Such conditions are necessary for the believer to experience a healthy spiritual life characterized by growth and development.

16. Why did God swear by himself (v. 13)? Does an oath always or usually increase confidence in what is said or promised? Explain.

27

17. What was God's promise to Abraham (v. 14)? In what ways does it apply to current believers? How did Abraham obtain the promise (v. 15)? What lesson can we learn from Abraham's example?

GOD'S OATH, OUR TRUST. 6:16-18

More solemn than men taking an oath before God is God's taking an oath before men. He seeks our faith. He wants to be trusted and believed. He cannot lie, yet He takes an oath to back up His promise.

18. According to verse 16, what is the purpose of an oath? Why did God confirm His promise to Abraham with an oath (v. 17)? What are the two unchangeable things mentioned in verses 17-18?

19. God sought a response from Abraham. What does He seek from humanity today? What is the relationship between faith, hope, and courage as they relate to the life of the believer (v. 18)? What advice would you give to people who are discouraged with life in general or some aspect of the Christian life in particular?

THE ANCHOR HOLDS. 6:19-20

20. What is the purpose of "hope" (v. 19)? In what way is spiritual drifting a danger to the believer? What really serves as an anchor for the soul? What is the significance of the phrase "inner sanctuary behind the curtain"?

21. According to verses 19-20 what has Jesus done for us? What does His action mean to you personally? What does verse 20 imply about the availability of Jesus to act as your High Priest?

INSIGHT/ACTION

22. What does Hebrews 6 teach you about the necessity of growth spiritually in the Christian life? What insights have you gained from your study of Hebrews 6 that will help you grow spiritually?

OPTIONAL ADVANCED STUDY

23. Select three persons in the Bible who were faithful to God in the face of opposition. Study them and describe in your study diary things that may have enabled them to grow spiritually in the face of opposition.

7 The Mystery Man

Read Hebrews 7

Everyone seems drawn to the mysterious. Most of us seem to have a built-in curiosity about many things.

The Bible contains many mysteries. In it we may find many things we don't understand but wish we did.

Hebrews 7 describes a mystery man. By studying this man and his character, we can begin to learn more about and appreciate in a deeper way God's Son — Jesus Christ.

WHO WAS THAT MASKED MAN? 7:1-3

Where have all the heroes gone? In the early days of radio and television there was a "western" hero who always waged war against lawlessness. He would subdue evil and ride off into the unknown. Right always triumphed. We need such a hero.

Rather than dwell in the realm of fantasy we can turn to Hebrews 7 and find a description of a "mystery man," Melchizedek, whose presence foreshadowed the coming of the perfect champion of right and justice — Jesus Christ.

Melchizedek is indeed one of the mystery men of the Bible. Little is known about him; the reference to him here in Hebrews is only the third and last time he is mentioned by the writer to the Hebrews. Melchizedek is first mentioned in Genesis 14:17-20.

1. According to verse 1 what was Melchizedek? Can you think of anyone else in the Bible who was both a "king" and "priest" and had God's approval? Explain.
2. What did Melchizedek do to Abraham (v. 1)? What does this act reveal about his position of power relative to Abraham? What did Abraham do (v. 2)? What does this act reveal about Abraham's perception of Melchizedek's religious position?
3. What two things does Melchizedek's name mean? In what ways might these two titles be appropriate titles for Jesus Christ?

29

4. What does verse 3 reveal about Melchizedek? Keeping in mind that this passage presents Melchizedek as a "foreshadow" or "type" of Christ's high priesthood, what does verse 3 mean? What point is being made about Jesus?
5. Consider the statement in the conclusion of verse 3. What does it mean to you personally to know Jesus Christ is a "priest forever"?

LITTLE KNOWN GREATNESS. 7:4-10

Although references to Melchizedek are very limited and he is a mysterious figure, he was great.

Remember, what may seem great to the world can be next to nothing in God's view. During His earthly life Jesus was a man of little known greatness. He touched many it is true and many were changed during the brief span of His ministry. But, He never ventured further than about a hundred miles from His home. Only a few of the total world population at the time recognized His greatness. However, as the resurrected Christ and High Priest in heaven, millions have recognized Him as their Savior and Lord.

6. Why do you think it was considered a sign of greatness to be in a position to receive tithes (v. 4)? What do you think prompted Abraham to offer Melchizedek a tenth of the spoils? What were tithes to be used for in the Mosaic system (v. 5)?
7. In what ways do verses 6-7 point out that Melchizedek (and Christ who was like him) was greater than Abraham? Is there any connection between blessings and tithes? Explain.
8. In what ways should a proper understanding of verses 4-10 contribute to the Christian virtue of humility?

GREATER THAN . . . 7:11-14

While on earth, Christ was often at odds with the religious establishment — the scribes and Pharisees. He opposed them because of their outward show of religiosity without anything even resembling the Spirit of God in their hearts. They had a form of worship but their hearts were far from God. Their priests were of Levitical heritage — descendants of Aaron the first high priest.

Now, one greater than Aaron had been among them. Jesus was a High Priest after the order of Melchizedek to whom even Aaron and his forefather Abraham had given tithes and been blessed.

9. What do you think is the basis for the statement in verse 7 that the Law and the Levitical priesthood was not "perfect"? What was the purpose of the Law and the priesthood? Was the Law ineffective in itself or in its handling or application by and through the priesthood?

10. On what value are written rules for regulating Christian conduct and life-style today?

11. Christ said He did not come to destroy the Law but to fulfill it (Matthew 5:17). In the light of this, what do you think is meant by the phrase, "When there is a change of the priesthood, there must also be a change of the Law"?

12. Summarize in one sentence the main message of verses 11-14. How does the abolishment of the priestly line and exaltation of Jesus to the role of heavenly High Priest affect all believers?

AN INDESTRUCTIBLE LIFE. 7:15-17

13. Upon what does Christ's priesthood rest (v. 16)? Do you think a majority of Christians barely scratch the surface in obtaining the power of the "indestructible life" that is available to them through Christ? Explain. If so, what hinders or holds them back?

14. What is revealed about Christ's priesthood (v. 17)? How should the assurance in verse 17 affect believers in times of doubt or uncertainty?

GUARANTEED. 7:18-22

15. Why do you think the writer continues to emphasize that the Law has been set aside (v. 18)? How does he describe it? Do believers today have problems in keeping works and grace in their proper perspective? Explain.

16. Who is the "better hope" (v. 19)? According to verse 19 what does this better hope allow us to do? In what way is the "better way" a new way to God in contrast with the old system? (Clue: How near to God did worshipers get during their worship in the Temple?)

17. According to verses 20-21, what supports the fact that Jesus is our High Priest? How does this knowledge affect your faith? For how long will He be a priest? How is Jesus described in verse 22?

ALWAYS ALIVE, ALWAYS ABLE. 7:23-25

18. Of what value is it to know that Jesus' priesthood is permanent (vv. 23-24)?

19. According to verse 25 what is Jesus able to do? What must we do to receive this benefit? Have you responded to this truth personally?

MEETING OUR NEED. 7:26-28

There is hope for anyone who feels a need. As we travel through life we can have the companionship of Jesus and the guidance of the Holy Spirit. These resources are available because Jesus is our High Priest and can meet our needs.

20. What does Christ do (v. 26)? List words from verse 26 that describe Christ. In what way is Jesus greater than previous high priests (vv. 27-28)? What has He done for you and all of humanity?

INSIGHT/ACTION

21. Review Hebrews 7. Summarize in a brief paragraph why Christ's priesthood is superior to the old order. Describe how you have taken advantage of Christ's offer to be your High Priest. Describe the ways you may have ignored or taken for granted His offer.

OPTIONAL ADVANCED STUDY

22. Use Bible commentaries and other resources to study the priesthood of the Old Testament, how it was set up, and the tasks and duties of the high priests. Contrast the priesthood of Christ with what you discover about the old system. How did Christ fulfill the Law?

8 Better Promises, Better Results

Read Hebrews 8

Life is full of promises. Sometimes, however, promises are broken and we find ourselves very disappointed. Promises, unless followed by actions and results, are useless and can even injure confidence and faith.

The writer to the Hebrews was very familiar with the promises God made to Israel, as was the audience he addressed. God's promises were conditional and the Israelites had not always kept their part. Their actions negatively affected fulfillment of the promises.

As you study Hebrews 8 you will discover a "new" and better promise from God — a promise that comes about not merely from an adherence to external codes, but from an internal heart obedience.

The promise is available to everyone through faith. This promise is Christ within, the hope of glory.

BY THE THRONE. 8:1-2

1. In what way is verse 1 a summary statement? What do we have and where is He? What does His position signify? Is Christ's present position "new" or is it reclaimed? Explain.
2. Define sanctuary (v. 2). Is heaven only a place or can it be a state of life if the kingdom of heaven is set up in the believer's heart by faith? What are some characteristics of the heavenly life in Jesus Christ as manifested by the Holy Spirit in the heart?
3. Describe the mood projected by the description given in verses 1 and 2.

Although the writer to the Hebrews has repeatedly emphasized Christ's position as both King and High Priest the need for repetition is evident, if you consider the circumstances faced by His audience.

The Hebrew Christians had accepted Christianity as an addition to their Levitical system of temple worship. Christ was a fuller revelation of God — an addition to their heritage and further proof of divine favor. They tried to combine their temple worship and Christianity.

However, this was not to be; the scribes and Pharisees saw to that. Persecution arose. The Hebrew believers were slowly but surely alienated from the temple worship. They were exempted from the great feast days and could not identify with the high priest in his ministry at the altar.

Some "believers" went back to the Jewish system — the pressure was too great. Others questioned if the Christian way was worth it.

The writer encouraged the Hebrew believers. They had not been deserted by God. They did indeed have a High Priest and a King in God's Son Jesus Christ.

4. Pretend for a moment you're a Hebrew believer facing what they faced. In what ways would knowing Christ as High Priest and King be an encouragement to hold firm to your new faith?

5. Are there situations today where believers because of their faith, face exclusion from groups to which they formerly belonged? Explain.

THE TRUE SANCTUARY. 8:3-5

6. According to verse 3 what is every high priest appointed to do? What do you think are the differences between "gifts and sacrifices"? To whom does the "this one" refer (v. 3)? What did He offer?

7. What do verses 4 and 5 compare and contrast? Define "sanctuary." In what ways might the earthly sanctuary have been a "copy and shadow"? What purpose did it serve? Are there things today that might "represent" God but are mere shadows of the real thing? Explain.

Sanctuaries are places where we can go to meet God. Today ministers often serve in sanctuaries to guide people in worship. Such sanctuaries are here because there is a true sanctuary in heaven. Earthly sanctuaries began when God told Moses to build a tabernacle patterned after the one in heaven. Jesus has returned to heaven and taken up the duties of a high priest in the heavenly sanctuary. He ministers there to impart the kingdom of heaven into our hearts as we live on earth.

8. Why was the doctrine of Jesus as a High Priest ministering in the true sanctuary in heaven good news for Hebrew Chris-

tians? Jesus is both King and High Priest. A king rules and has power. What is the purpose of a high priest and what does he represent?

9. Jesus serving in the sanctuary in heaven held special meaning for the Hebrew believers. He also serves in the sanctuary within — the heart of the believer. What does this imply about the body of the believer? Explain.

10. Moses received his instructions from God while alone on a mountain. What are some ways you have received guidance from God? Are there benefits of solitary communion with God? Explain.

MEDIATOR NEEDED. 8:6-9

The Hebrews could relate to the covenant concept in God's dealing with humanity. Such a relationship had begun for them with the covenant God had made with Abraham and continued with Moses. Now the Old Covenant was to be replaced and a new mediator appointed. The New Covenant included better promises and guaranteed better results — righteousness and holiness in living.

11. What is the main emphasis of verse 6? In what ways is His ministry superior to that of the Levitical high priest? What makes the New Covenant superior to the Old? What are the "better promises" on which the New Covenant is founded?

12. What appears to have been the downfall of the Old Covenant (vv. 8-9)? Was the Old Covenant externally or internally based? Explain. What were the consequences to those under the Old Covenant for rejecting or being unfaithful to God? Are there similar changes under the New Covenant relationship? Explain. How can these dangers be avoided.

THE BIG CHANGE. 8:10-11

13. To what does the phrase "after that time" refer (v. 10)? Is the covenant explained in verse 10 internal or external? Explain. With whom is the covenant made? In what ways are people in addition to Jews included in this promise?

35

14. Compare Jeremiah 31:31-34 with Hebrews 8:10-11. In what ways are the passages similar?
15. Is it possible merely to follow God with one's "will" without having a total "heart" commitment to Him (v. 10)? If so, why is such an approach less than ideal?
16. Describe what you think it means to "Know the Lord" (v. 11).

FORGIVEN AND FORGOTTEN. 8:12-13

Forgiveness is at the heart of the New Testament. We find it in all the teachings and actions of Jesus.

17. What two things will the Lord do according to verse 12? Why is it a comfort to know God will not "remember" our sins in addition to "forgiving" our sins? How is verse 12 a good model for us to follow when someone wrongs us?
18. In what two ways is the Old Covenant described in verse 13? What has caused this action to occur? Do you have a covenant relationship with Christ (personal)? Upon what is your relationship based?

The "better way" founded on better promises provides better results. The results are like three peas in a pod: (a) pardon of sin by which the very thought of our sin is put out of the heart (memory) of God; (b) purity of heart in which the love of sin is put out of our heart; (c) and the presence of God in which the heavenly life (living within the veil) is imparted to our hearts by the Holy Spirit.

INSIGHT/ACTION

19. Review Hebrews 8. Based on this passage, describe in a brief paragraph the main advantages you see for you personally in the New Covenant in contrast with the Old Covenant.

OPTIONAL ADVANCED STUDY

20. Search the New Testament for promises available under the New Covenant. List in your study diary as many as you can find. Bible handbooks and other Bible references may provide lists of such promises. Make copies of the list of promises you found (along with the correct scripture references) and share them with friends.

9 Shadows from the Sanctuary

Read Hebrews 9:1-10

We are all familiar with symbolism. We encounter symbols each day. Think of common examples such as organization letterheads or company logos. Symbols are designed to carry connotative meanings. They stand for something.

Symbols can also be used to represent spiritual things. Churches are full of symbols. Common examples include the cross, praying hands, and a white dove.

One Old Testament symbol of Christ and His work is found in the Tabernacle. Various items in and the design of the Tabernacle pointed toward the Messiah and what He would do.

As you study Hebrews 9:1-10 you will gain many insights into the person and work of Jesus Christ represented in the Tabernacle.

DESIGN AND RITUAL. 9:1-5

The Tabernacle was made for a purpose. God's instructions to Moses were, "Then have them make a sanctuary for me, and I will dwell among them. Make this tabernacle and all its furnishings exactly like the pattern I will show you" (Exodus 25:8-9). Under the Old Covenant, the sanctuary was the place where the presence of God resided among His people. The design had spiritual significance and each component was expressive of some truth to be fully revealed in Jesus Christ the Redeemer.

1. What two things are listed as part of the First Covenant (v. 1)? Do you think there is any significance in use of the word "earthly" to describe the sanctuary? Explain. Why do you think "regulations" for worship were included in the First Covenant? What purpose were they to fulfill?

When a worshiper approached the Tabernacle he came to the sacred walls of an oblong, roofless enclosure. The walls were composed of pillars of brass five cubits apart upon which canvas screens were hung. These walls formed the outer court of the Tabernacle (about 150 feet long and 75 feet wide). The height of the wall was seven and one-half feet. The Tabernacle was pitched with its length from east to west with its only opening on the east end. The entrance was overhung with "fine twined linen" wrought with needlework and made up of gorgeous colors. The linen represented the righteousness of Christ. The colors were blue, purple, and scarlet. Blue signified the heavenly character of Christ, purple represented His royalty, and scarlet His suffering and shed blood.

The actual Tabernacle inside the court was located to the rear of the enclosure and was 45 feet long, 15 feet wide, and 15 feet high at the walls. It was made of Acacia wood, overlaid with gold. The boards were upright, placed edge to edge and fitted in sockets of silver at the bottom. The corners were coupled with rings and the roof was probably stretched across a ridgepole like on a tent. The roof was made of rams' skins dyed red and of badgers' skins. Even the roof was symbolic of the blood that covers the sins of the repentant.

The Tabernacle had two rooms. The first was the Holy Place. To the rear and separated by a thick curtain or veil was a smaller room — the Holy of Holies or most Holy Place.

> 2. What was the first room in the Tabernacle called (v. 2)? What did it contain?

The lampstand foreshadowed the church and Christ as the Light of the World. The bread pointed forward to Christ's body sacrificed for the life of sinful man. Also some commentators suggest that within the Holy Place there was possibly an altar of incense. From this altar live coals may have been taken for the burning of incense in a censer inside the Most Holy Place. The burning of this incense symbolized the prayer for sins of ignorance by the priests and the people, and the prayer for forgiveness of the high priest carrying out the ceremony.

> 3. Do "believers" today surround themselves with things that are spiritual symbols? If so, what purpose do they serve? Is there any chance the symbols could take the place of what they stand for? Explain.
> 4. What was located behind the second curtain (v. 3)? What was contained in this area (v. 4)? Why do you think the author of Hebrews decided not to discuss the items in detail (v. 5)?

The Most Holy Place was a cubical room measuring ten cubits each way (about fifteen feet). The veil leading to the Most Holy Place was of the same material and color as that of the Tabernacle entrance and the eastern gate to the outer court. Again the veil symbolizes the way into God's presence is through the work of Christ.

The golden altar of incense (v. 4) was made of Acacia wood overlaid with pure gold. This golden altar stood immediately before the veil, behind which was the Most Holy Place. The altar was used to burn incense. But, it is thought incense was burned on coals in a censer that was extended by the high priest through the veil into the Most Holy Place on the Day of Atonement. The smoke from the incense represented prayers and permeated the Most Holy Place before the high priest dared to enter.

For more information about the items listed in the Most Holy Place note the following references: Ark of the Covenant (Exodus 25:10-22); golden jar of manna (Exodus 16:32-34); Aaron's budded rod (Numbers 17:1-10); the cherubim (Exodus 25:17-22; 37:6-9).

Sacrificial blood was sprinkled on the golden lid of the ark by the high priest on the Day of Atonement.

5. Verses 1-5 imply a great deal of preparation was involved in coming into the presence of God? What are some ways believers can and should prepare to worship God?

6. Based on the contents of verses 1-5 what one-word description would you give to the Tabernacle and all it contained? In many ways the contents of the Most Holy Place represented God's revelation to His people in the past. Why is it good to save memories or momentos of God's past blessing to us? How did these items of Israel's past point toward the future?

TABERNACLE WORSHIP. 9:6-7

7. Briefly outline the order of worship given in verses 6-7. For what was blood used (v. 7)?

The Tabernacle design and furnishings all pointed to the Messiah, Jesus Christ. Tabernacle worship, beyond question, was the greatest prophetic expression of the redemptive work of Christ.

The worshiper, sorry for his sins, brought his sacrifice to the great altar of burnt offerings just inside the gate. He tied it to the horns of the altar and then laid his hands on the animal's head, thereby transferring the guilt of the sins upon it, as the priest killed the innocent victim. The blood of the sacrifice was shed, its flesh consumed on the altar. As the worshiper beheld the smoke of his sacrifice rising heavenward he had the divine assurance that his sins had been canceled at the price of the life of an innocent one.

8. The Israelite came to the altar with a sacrifice. Could he place trust in his offering? Explain. Do would-be believers (sinners seeking forgiveness) have any offering to bring to the altar? What can such a person claim as his offering for sins?

LIMITATIONS. 9:8-10

9. According to verse 8 what was the Holy Spirit doing through the worship procedure in the Tabernacle? What was wrong with the gifts and offerings of the worshiper (v. 9)? What purpose did tabernacle worship fulfill (v. 10)?
10. We are now in the "new order" (v. 10). In a brief paragraph describe how and why worship of God is different today.
11. The Hebrews knew well the order of tabernacle worship. Why do you think the writer took time to go over the worship with which they were so familiar? Is there any danger today of getting so used to an order of worship that we really fail to worship? Explain.

INSIGHT/ACTION

12. In what ways can an understanding of tabernacle worship help us better understand Christ's role in granting forgiveness for sin today?
13. Under the "new order" Christ is our intercessor. He is the gate to restored fellowship with God. Examine your life. Have you taken advantage of the "new order" and the access it provides to God? How can you completely worship God?

OPTIONAL ADVANCED STUDY

14. Use your Bible and additional Bible study resources to study the building of both Solomon's and Herod's temples as permanent sanctuaries of worship. Record in your study diary how closely they followed God's directions for the Tabernacle. Also list the blessings these temples added to the nation of Israel, and the changes that arose. Think about ways in which similar dangers and blessings may apply to church structures today.

10 The Blood of Christ

Read Hebrews 9:11 — 10:18

As the sun sets behind the mountains in northern New Mexico, a strange phenomenon takes place. In the last rays of the sun, the majestic peaks radiate a distinct red tint. Because of this display which has occurred for centuries, priests who accompanied early Spanish explorers named the range of mountains Sangre de Cristo meaning "the blood of Christ." The explorers sought gold. They found little or none. Yet the mountains and their name remains, a testimony of the Savior's blood worth more than any gold. The power of Christ's blood and its affect on human hearts will still endure even when the Sangre de Cristo range has ceased to be or there is no sun to make them blood red.

As you study this session you will discover how Christ's death and the shedding of His blood provides a way for each of us to find forgiveness for sin and acceptance before God.

THE BLOOD, ETERNAL REDEMPTION. 9:11-12

The scripture for this session (9:11 — 10:18) concludes the doctrinal portion of the letter to the Hebrews. These verses contain the very heart of Christian doctrine — that is the sacrifice of the body and blood of the sinless Son of God, Jesus Christ, to take away the sin principle from the heart, and to cancel the penalty for sins committed. What Adam lost in the Fall, the Son, the Second Adam (I Corinthians 15:45-49) regains through the sacrifice of himself. The sacrifices of the Mosaic system had pointed to the perfect sacrifice. It was part of God's eternal plan of redemption. The blood of bulls and goats pointed worshipers to One in whom they could have faith for forgiveness and cleansing. Through the blood of Christ eternal redemption had been obtained.

1. Verse 11 states, ". . . Christ came a high priest of the good things that are already here. . . ." What were the good things? What does this reveal about the writer's doctrinal position and attitude toward the Levitical system?

41

2. What is ". . . the greater and more perfect tabernacle that is not man-made, that is to say, not a part of this creation" (v. 11) that Christ went through? How does this aid in the acceptance of spiritual worship to replace ritualistic forms and symbolism?

3. What does the expression ". . . he entered the Most Holy Place once for all . . ." convey to you (v. 12)? Does the "for all" refer to people or express a finality about entering the Most Holy Place only once? Explain.

THE BLOOD, CLEANSING POWER. 9:13-14

In the language of the Bible the blood stands for life. The Hebrews thought that the life of a man or animal was actually contained in the blood. That is why they spoke of the blood of a murdered man crying for vengeance from the ground (note, Genesis 4:10). It follows, then, that the references to the blood of Christ mean the life of Christ given for us. When we say the blood of Christ cleanses us from all sin, we mean His life given for us does this.

4. What is life? When does it begin? Compare and contrast physical and spiritual life.

5. What is the importance of Christ's statement ". . . I have come that they may have life, and have it to the full" (John 10:10)? In what ways can you relate this verse to the mysteries in the phrase ". . . his own blood" (v. 12)? How can we have "full" life in His blood?

6. What was the purpose of ceremonial sanctification (v. 13)? Could it instill life? What was its value?

The sacrifice of Jesus Christ according to the writer to the Hebrews in verse 14 was distinctive in four points. First, it was the offering of a person by himself — it was self-sacrifice. Secondly, the person was blameless. Thirdly, it was a spiritual sacrifice; it was in the realm of the spirit he offered himself. And lastly, it was by and through the instrument of the Holy Spirit — the eternal Spirit — gaining eternal redemption.

7. Compare and contrast verses 13 and 14. How was Christ offered as a sacrifice for sin? What cleansing effect does the

blood (Christ within) have? What is the nature of the service implied in "... so that we may serve the living God"?

8. What is basically wrong with the current humanistic approach to man's efforts in trying to improve himself and the world order? What truths expressed in verse 14, if embraced, would revolutionize mankind?

9. What are the characteristics of a conscience subjected to the cleansing blood of Christ which can "... cleanse our conscience from acts that lead to death ..." (v. 14)?

THE BLOOD, LEGACY OF LOVE. 9:15-22

God planned for us. He made a New Covenant — a will — sealed by the blood of His own Son. And Jesus is the Mediator to assure that we are recipients of the full benefits of the heavenly life through himself. We have a legacy of love.

10. What is the usual opening language of a will made by a person to dispose of his possessions after death? One Greek word is translated "covenant," "testament," or "will," depending on the word's context in Scripture. What are the common characteristics of each?

11. What is the significance of the word "promised" in verse 15? Who was the promise for (note Acts 2:39)?

12. What lives were given to keep the First Covenant in effect (verses 18-21)? What was the ultimate basis for the forgiveness of sins even under the First Covenant (v. 15)?

One of the greatest doctrinal assertions of the New Testament is "... without the shedding of blood there is no forgiveness" (v. 22). This is the heart of the gospel — Christ died for sinners. Without the shedding of blood there is no blessing. The word "bless" is derived from the old Anglo-Saxon word for blood. The blood of Christ is our blessing. Christ said, "Greater love has no one than this, that one lay down his life for his friends" (John 15:13). We cannot atone, but we can bless. We may not shed blood literally, but we can share in the sufferings of fellow believers — and love them.

43

13. In what ways can we know and share in the sufferings of others?
14. Define "atonement." There are religious teachers who reject atonement through the blood as being coarse and at variance with a finer culture such as ours. How can a proper understanding of this doctrine of atonement through the shed blood of Christ dispel these criticisms?

THE BLOOD, FUTURE FORTUNE. 9:23-28

If we sometimes lose contentment with our lot in life, verses 23-28 should help us to see that as believers our hope is in Christ. He is now ministering in heaven for us, having done away with our sin by the sacrifice of himself. And He's coming back! Our future fortune rests secure in the blood — the life of Christ — which treasure we have within and our affections are on things above. What a future we have! "When Christ, who is your life, appears, then you also will appear with him in glory" (Colossians 3:4).

15. What do you think is the meaning of the statement that the need for purifying extended to ". . . the heavenly things themselves with better sacrifices than these" (v. 23)? In what sense were the heavenly things unclean or in need of the blood of Christ?
16. Christ is in the presence of God for us (v. 24) and from there imparts the heavenly life. In what ways may we as Christians fail to claim the fullness of the life offered? Can you be an heir to great privileges and not actually inherit them? Explain.
17. How would you describe the finality of the statement that Christ ". . . has appeared once for all at the end of the ages to do away with sin by the sacrifice of himself" (v. 26)?

In the closing verses of chapter 9 three appearings of Jesus Christ are mentioned. These cover three distinct stages of the work of our Redeemer: He has appeared on earth and finished His work to destroy the works of the devil, to put away sin by the sacrifice of himself (v. 26), He does now appear in the presence of God in heaven to break the constraining and compelling power of sin (v. 24), and He will appear openly and visibly on earth again to remove those who are waiting for Him. The waiting ones are not sinners for He is not coming to "bear sin" (v. 28).

18. Christ put away sin by His self-sacrifice. In what ways must every person choose between sin and self or Christ and His self? Can sin be defined as a refusal to sacrifice one's self to God? Explain. What is involved in self-sacrifice to God?
19. What is the destiny of all humanity (v. 27)? Pascal once remarked, "I shall be alone in death." Is such an idea useful and valid? Explain. Does preparing for death add some common sense to life? How does one best prepare?
20. What attitudes should one have toward the plain statement that we are to die and then ". . . face judgment" (v. 27)? Do Christians have an apprehension about the judgment? Explain.
21. What is the great hope extended to believers in verse 28? In what manner should we be found ". . . waiting for him" (note also Luke 12:37-40)?

ANIMAL SACRIFICES, ANNUAL REMINDERS. 10:1-7

The Law given to Moses was a true revelation of the will of God for that time and dispensation. It revealed God's plan of redemption as much as it was possible to do then. Its precepts set forth what God demanded of men and expected of them. If its precepts were fulfilled, men might set themselves right with God. Righteousness under the Mosaic system was defined as keeping the precepts of the Law. But in actuality no man was ever able to fulfill its demands, and consequently there was never true peace of heart or a good conscience. Yearly animal sacrifices only served as annual reminders that the heart longed for and needed something more from God. The Apostle Paul testified to the failure of the Law. He had found neither righteousness nor peace even though with all the passion of his soul he had given himself to observe every detail of the Law. Then he met Jesus and found in Him the reality of which the Law was but a shadow. In Christ and His cross Paul found the righteousness, reconciliation, and the peace of a good conscience he had sought. His elusive longing was now reality and he cried out, "Thanks be to God . . . !" (Romans 7:25).

22. The epistle to the Hebrews deals much with types and shadows of realities to come (10:1). Is there a sense in which

all our lives are shadows? Explain. Does eternity hold for the believer a promise for full development and realization of the potentialities of the soul (note I Corinthians 13:12)?

23. All of us will undoubtedly die with some tasks unfinished and ideals unrealized. What are some of your personal goals for which eternity provides hope of fulfillment?

24. Review Hebrews 10:1-3 and list the failures of the Levitical system of worship. What were some of the frustrations worshipers faced? The writer characterizes the sacrifices as ". . . an annual reminder of sins . . ." (10:3). What purpose does a reminder without a remedy serve?

25. Explain the prophecy concerning Christ in Psalm 40:6-8 (Hebrews 10:5-7). What was it God didn't desire? What did Christ have to offer? What can the body be used for? Is obedience always better than repentance or sacrifice (Luke 22:42; I Samuel 15:22)? Explain.

SINLESS BODY, PERFECT SACRIFICE. 10:8-18

These verses conclude the doctrinal portion of the epistle. Attention will now be focused on practical living — holiness in the crucible of life. The lengthy discourse showing how Christ was the substance of the Law had been essential; all had pointed to Him. Effectiveness of the Law relied on Christ's coming into the world in a sinless embodiment of God, and then using that body willingly as the perfect sacrifice for sin. He came to be one of us without sin that we might be like Him — without sin.

26. According to verse 9, Jesus set aside the First Covenant to establish the Second. What did you set aside, or may yet be in the process of setting aside, to do God's will?

27. Is it possible for activities associated with Christianity (going to services, reading the Word, prayer,) to become mere religious duties, ". . . again and again he offers the same sacrifices . . ." (v. 11)? If so, what's the remedy?

28. What does the expression, ". . . he has made perfect forever those who are being made holy" (v. 14) mean? How do the quotations from Jeremiah 31:33, 34 help explain the part played by the Holy Spirit (vv. 15-16)?
29. After sins have been forgiven what is the meaning of the tremendous closing doctrinal statement, ". . . there is no longer any sacrifice for sin" (v. 18)?

INSIGHT/ACTION

30. Based on insights you have gained from your study of Hebrews 9:11 — 10:18 describe why Christ provides a better way to be restored to God than does mere obedience to the Law.
31. Since Christ gave His life for you, in what ways can you give your life to Him?

ADVANCED OPTIONAL STUDY

32. Use a family or home medical guide book. Review the section on human blood: what is the function of blood, what are some diseases and disorders of the blood? The conclusion follows that the human body cannot be healthy without healthy blood. Now take your Bible concordance and find scriptures which support the doctrine of redemption for mankind through the blood of Christ. The conclusion follows that the church — the body — is only alive and healthy as it accepts and retains faith in the blood of Christ. Record your insights in your study diary.
33. Select from Hebrews 9:11 — 10:18 verses for memorization.

11 Spiritual Passage

Read Hebrews 10:19 — 11:34

Life is in constant motion. It moves in constant progression which is marked by various rites of passage. Birthdays, anniversaries, and various celebrations are ways we often measure time.

Our spiritual lives also contain milestones. Once the basics of the Christian life have been learned we must move on to their application in life. We enter another sphere of the Christian life — the life of holiness.

By faith we find the cleansing and strength needed to live responsibly our lives as part of a royal priesthood and the holy family.

THE CHALLENGE OF FAITH. 10:19-25

The failure of most religions is in the matter of living. Many have precepts and doctrines which sound good. Generally most people know that they should live differently, on a higher moral and spiritual plane. Power is lacking to live what doctrine dangles before needy humanity. Christianity provides the power. It is a challenge of faith to every believer to claim all God has provided through Jesus Christ. The very presence and power of God from within the Holy of Holies can be a reality within the heart of every believer. From outside the Tabernacle, as it were, we may proceed into the presence of God and there live. Failure usually is in faith to claim our place. Too many for too long are "outer court" Christians. They stay near to the outside world with its commerce and merchandising which Christ condemned when he drove the money changers from the outer court of the Temple (Matthew 21:12). Others are "temple proper" Christians. They are into the stately, formal, ritualistic mode of worship with a dependency on others to lead them in worship. The challenge of faith is to be a "Holy of Holies" Christian — to claim our position as a priest unto God, and talk and fellowship with Him in the Most Holy Place. And we are temples. His residence is our hearts — our lives an expression of Jesus Christ within. That's practical holiness at work.

1. According to verses 19-21 what great blessings does Christianity provide for worship and living which were not possible under the Old Covenant? Explain the significance of the opening of the Most Holy Place and the confidence (boldness) which we may have to enter it. How is the way into the Most Holy Place described? Who is within the sanctuary and what is His work?

2. What four things does God seek from believers as they come to Him in true worship (v. 22)? What do you think is meant by "a sincere heart"? What is involved in "full assurance of faith"? Is it for every believer? Explain. What advantage do we have for living a successful Christlike life by being cleansed "from a guilty conscience" (the thought of sin in our hearts) by the sprinkling of blood. To what do you think the phrase "having our bodies washed with pure water" refers? Why is such an outer cleansing important?

3. The Christian is called to four duties (expressed as "Let us . . .") made possible when Christ opened the veil to the Holy of Holies. How can we best: (a) comply with the duty to ". . . draw near to God with a sincere heart in full assurance of faith" (v. 22), (b) ". . . hold unswervingly to the hope we profess . . ." (v. 23), (c) ". . . spur one another on toward love and good deeds" (v. 24), and (d) assure we do not ". . . give up meeting together . . . encourage one another . . . as you see the Day approaching" (v. 25)? What do you think a keeping of these duties does for Christians individually and collectively?

THE RUINATION OF FAITH. 10:26-31

We come now to the fourth warning in the epistle to the Hebrews. In the three previous warnings the writer had spoken of neglect (2:1-4), unbelief and disobedience (3:1 — 4:13), and sloth (5:13 — 6:19). The entrance to the Holy of Holies has been opened for all. But the awful truth remains that the gate of hell is also opened wide to receive any and all who deliberately or through neglect refuse to choose the narrow way of righteousness of which Jesus Christ is the gate (Matthew 7:13-14; John 10:1-9).

4. Just prior to sounding the warning the writer mentioned those who "... give up meeting together" (v. 25). When and in what way does neglect of Christian fellowship become dangerous? Can it lead to the terrible condition that is described as to "... deliberately keep on sinning ..." (v. 26)? Explain.

5. What do you think is meant by verse 26? Is it another way of expressing the "unpardonable sin" described by Jesus (Mark 3:29)? Does "... after we have received the knowledge of the truth ..." mean being regenerated or is it just believing with the head? Explain. What do you think is meant by "... no sacrifice for sin is left"? Compare and contrast verse 26 with verse 18.

6. What does verse 28 reveal about the punishment reserved for those who broke the law of Moses under the Old Covenant? What do you think the writer was trying to say in verse 29?

7. How does one trample "... the Son of God under foot"; treat the blood of Christ as being unclean when it has "... sanctified him" (cleansed him from sin); and insult the Spirit of grace?

8. In what ways might it be difficult for the human mind to fully grasp the judgment of an angry God described in verses 30-31?

REMEMBRANCE AND RESOLVE IN FAITH. 10:32-39

The ability to remember can be a great blessing. As we grow older we are more inclined to remember the good years, the vitality we had, the blessings we received from God, the hard times that taught us lessons of faith, and the commitments we made. These remembrances can encourage us in the faith and help us resolve to press on in the Christian life. God has helped! He will continue to be our help and strength.

9. For what does the writer to the Hebrews commend the believers in verses 32-34? Why do you think he tells them to remember their stand for Christ in the past? Will the very best of Christian beginnings avail nothing unless we endure to the end? Explain.

10. What does the writer tell his readers to do (v. 35)? Why are they to persevere (v. 36)? In what ways should verse 37 be an encouragement to believers?

11. By what shall the righteous live (v. 38)? Based on verses 38-39 what will happen to those who do not persevere in the faith? What will happen to those who believe?

FAITH, THE FOUNDATION. 11:1-3

Bishop Lightfoot used to say: "If we could only discover a large number of business documents and ordinary correspondence which were written at the time the New Testament was being written, we might come to quite a new and rich interpretation of many of the New Testament words." What he hoped for happened. Large quantities of business documents and ordinary correspondence dating to the Apostolic days were and are being found. These use words which the Apostle Paul used in his epistles. A word describing faith which has been translated in Hebrews 11:1 as "being sure" and "substance" (KJV) is found in first century documents. How is it used there? The common usage was in reference to buying or selling a house and the word is equivalent to the content of what we would call a "title deed." Many believe the writer to the Hebrews had this concept in mind when he sought to convey the wonderful concept of Christian faith. There are vast moral and spiritual estates available to every child of God. We hope to advance and achieve higher spiritual graces. If we accept them, they are ours now. We stand with "title deed" in hand.

12. Define faith according to verse 1. Describe in your own words what you think makes up faith. Contrast faith and opinion.

FAITH'S FAMOUS. 11:4-34

There have been many great and famous persons in God's hall of fame. The Bible contains a gallery of them. They had one thing in common — faith in God. They are examples from which much can be learned in our walk by faith.

13. Describe what you think was the secret of Abel's immortality in that "... he still speaks, even though he is dead" (v. 4)? What part did faith play in Enoch's triumph of life over death (vv. 5-6)? In what way was Noah's ark a work of faith (v. 7)? What prompted his building — fear, faith, or both? Explain. What was the end result?

14. What great characteristic of faith did Abraham exemplify (vv. 8-19)? Is there a sense in which all persons of faith, all Christians, have a "pilgrim spirit" (v. 13)? Define a "pilgrim."

15. Explain the consequences of Moses' decision of faith (vv. 23-30). How can his experiences enchance our faith? What part does individual choice play in faith?

16. Why do you think Rahab the prostitute was included among the famous (v. 31)? In what way is she an example of the power of faith to change lives? What did she risk based only on hope or faith?

17. The writer mentions a few prominent judges, kings, and prophets (vv. 32-34). What were their achievements? Is faith at its best when faced with difficulty and danger? Explain. How closely were the achievements of faith identified with the public welfare? Is selfishness the death of faith? How does sanctification deal with selfishness?

INSIGHT/ACTION

18. What has Hebrews 10:19 — 11:34 revealed to you about the importance of faith and perseverance in the faith?

19. Select one character from the listing of characters in Hebrews chapter 11 who appeals to you. What help can this person's example give you today to continue to have faith?

OPTIONAL ADVANCED STUDY

20. The writer ran out of space to tell about the faith exploits of Gideon, Barak, Samson, Jephthah, David, and Samuel (v. 32). Review accounts of them in the Bible. List in your study diary their background, special abilities, training, and limitations. How did faith in God shape and control their accomplishments? Were they like us? A little or a lot?

12 From Faith, Hope

Read Hebrews 11:35 — 12:29

God never promised believers would have a life free from trouble. How do you react when life becomes difficult?

The believer must remember his life is yoked to Christ and fix his gaze on the hope Jesus offers. The holy life is one of discipline. Although all believers enjoy special times of emotional stirring when the presence of God seems near, holiness goes even deeper than emotion and the sanctified believer can find true hope even during times when emotional tides subside and feelings fade.

During the study of this lesson you will discover that faith need not waver even in the most difficult circumstances.

REMEMBER WHEN. 11:35-40

The author of Hebrews began chapter 11 with a general overview of faith as the one element necessary to follow God. As chapter 11 closes, he cites specific examples of faith throughout history and underscores God's commendation of their courage and His promise of an inevitable fitting reward.

1. List the specific examples of faith recorded in verses 35-38. Have you ever complained about how difficult it was to follow Christ personally? How does persecution of believers in our society compare to the description in verses 35-38?

2. Why do you think the author included examples (vv. 35-38) of those who in faith triumphed over suffering? Can blessing and spiritual growth be obtained through suffering? Explain.

3. How do verses 35-38 compare to the teaching of some false teachers who promise material prosperity to all who follow Christ? In what way is faith as necessary in bearing temporary defeat as in securing victory? What do you think is meant by the phrase "the world was not worthy of them" (v. 38)? What do verses 39-40 reveal about the believer's receipt of the promised reward?

WITNESS, WEIGHTS, AND WONDERS. 12:1-3

Chapter 12 begins with one of the Bible's significant "therefore's." The Hebrew Christians were being severely tested. The writer appealed to the past and listed saints or martyrs who lived by faith and were victors. Although these martyrs were not spared from trials and suffering they could claim victory and served as witnesses and an encouragement in faith to the Hebrew believers who followed.

4. What do you think is meant by the phrase "a great cloud of witnesses" (v. 1)?

The Greek word used in verse 1 for witnesses refers to those who "testify to a truth or fact."

5. In what ways can the testimony of faithful "saints" from the past encourage us to persevere in faith today?
6. Describe what you think is included in "throw off everything that hinders . . ." ("Let us lay aside every weight," KJV) in verse 1? Describe what you think "the sin" means in this verse. What is the "race" referred to in verse 1?
7. How should we run our race (vv. 1-3)? What does it mean to you personally to know that Christ is "the author and perfecter of our faith"? According to verse 3, what advice is given to avoid weariness and loss of heart? Describe ways you can "fix" your gaze on Christ.

According to one commentator, the word "consider" (v. 3) means "careful and reflective comparison or weighing of matters."

THE ROD, RIGHTEOUSNESS, AND REST. 12:4-13

Discipline, righteousness, peace and holiness are interrelated. Indeed, the measure of our Christian perfection is directly related to our discipline in self-denial, prayer and fasting. Even Christ in His suffering found through it spiritual glory for ". . . he learned obedience from what He suffered . . ." (Hebrews 5:8).

8. How is the believer's relationship to sin described (v. 4)? What do you think is meant by the phrase "resisted to the point of shedding your blood"? Do all Christians "struggle" against sin? Explain.

9. What do you think is the purpose of the author's quoting Proverbs 3:11, 12 (v. 5-6)? What do verses 5-6 reveal about the Lord's discipline of us?

10. How are we to endure hardship (v. 7)? What is the purpose of discipline for the believer (vv. 7-10)? Since salvation is by grace through faith (Ephesians 2:8) why do you think suffering is suggested in this passage as a natural part of a believer's life?

11. Is there any reason for Christians to act like chastisement from God doesn't hurt? Explain. What lesson is there for believers in the statement that "... later on, however, it produces a harvest of righteousness and peace for those who have been trained by it" (v. 11)?

12. In what way is despondency or feelings of inadequacy dealt with in verses 12 and 13?

PEACE, PURITY, AND PERCEPTION. 12:14

The thought of so many who fail in the pursuit of holiness and return to the old life apparently causes the writer of Hebrews to abruptly interrupt his instructions for living the Christian life. He now gives the fifth and last warning before proceeding to the subject of love and good works which concludes the epistle. The fifth warning is introduced by a verse (12:14) often used as a text for sermons on holiness. The verse begins, "Make every effort to live in peace with all men. . . ." My relationship with other human beings is intimately one with my relationship to God. They are also His creation and objects of His concern.

13. What does verse 14 tell us to do? From what source does peace and holiness originate? What warning is given in verse 14? Define holiness. How can you have a pure heart and what are the benefits of having one? There can be no peace until we first are at peace with God. A pure and holy God desires His people to be holy. Sanctification is literally "holy making" or making pure. Holy making is the spiritual preparation, the inner capacity for meeting the Lord and being

at home with Him. It is the losing of self and being filled with the Spirit and likeness of Jesus. In Him we find purity. Our perception of God grows clearer as we surrender ourselves to His will and are made perfect in His love.

ATTITUDES, ACTS, AND ASSEMBLIES. 12:15-29

The last warning sounded by the writer is concerning backsliding. Such a warning was timely then and is also now. One may start in the race and fail to finish. There are so many distractions. Our attitudes, acts, and peers can hinder and hold us back. On the other hand, by and through being made holy our actions, attitudes and the assemblies of past saints and angels now enable us to finish the race. We follow Jesus the forerunner. Others have followed Him and made it. So can we. Make every effort. Victory is in sight.

14. According to verse 15 what are our responsibilities to others relative to ". . . the grace of God . . ."? What are some practical ways we can help others?

15. Three dangers that are causes and marks of missing the grace of God are listed in verses 15-17. What are they? What are some contemporary examples of "bitter root" things? How can they be avoided? In what way and why is sexual immorality a special hazard in our society? Esau lost spiritual discernment and sold out to temporary material satisfaction. Does such danger exist today? Explain.

16. Contrast and compare the Mount Sinai experience (vv. 18-21) with the Mount Zion experience (vv. 22-24). What is the mood expressed in verses 22-24? How can you be part of the scene described in these verses? Have you taken advantage of the opportunity (personal)?

17. What warning is given in verse 25? Where is the kingdom referred to in verse 28?

18. How should we respond to being part of such an unshakable kingdom (v. 28)? In what way is God a "consuming fire"? In what way does God as a "consuming fire" help us remain pure and live successful Christlike lives?

INSIGHT/ACTION

19. Review Hebrews 11:35 — 12:29. List in your own words the guidelines this passage gives for successful daily living for Christ, and for completing life's race through all circumstances.
20. What advantage is there in knowing that God's kingdom is internal rather than external in the world?

OPTIONAL ADVANCED STUDY

21. The letter to the Hebrews (KJV) uses the word "perfect" fourteen times. Use a concordance and list the use of this word in Hebrews and in other books in the New Testament.
22. Select and memorize from Hebrews 11:35 — 12:29 verses that are especially meaningful to you.

13 Unbroken Love

Read Hebrews 13

Learning is a never-ending process. The more we know, the more we begin to see how little we know. This same truth also applies to the spiritual as well as the physical. Learning all there is to know about God and His love will take this lifetime and more. The letter to the Hebrews helps draw back the curtain of the spiritual unknown and helps us gain deeper spiritual knowledge.

The inspired writer to the Hebrews gives us a doctrinal exposition of redemption through Christ and His fulfillment of the Law and Levitical worship that is unparalleled anywhere in the New Testament. He sounds five warnings or reproofs, corrects errors and misconceptions, and provides instruction for Christian living.

As you have studied Hebrews you have discovered Christ is the "better way." Through the power of the Spirit we can live consistent Christlike lives. As you study Hebrews 13 you will gain important insights on how the truths of Christianity really apply to life every day.

HOLINESS AND HARMONY. 13:1

1. What instruction is given in verse 1? What does the word "keep" suggest about the action to be taken? Describe in your own words what you think it means to love someone like a "brother."

Christ gave us the concept of brotherhood in God. God is our Father. Believers are brothers. God is love and within His presence we cannot but fulfill Christ's instruction ". . . Love each other as I have loved you" (John 15:12). Jesus was not ashamed to call us brothers (Hebrews 2:11). So we love each other and are one as brothers in Christ. This does not mean we are all identical — not clones. Brothers have their differences in personalities and opinions. There may at times be disagreement and dissent, but love and harmony of purpose remain.

2. In what way is "loving each other as brothers" a true test of the reality of our faith? What are some examples of ways we can "love our brothers"? Should the expression of the love within extend beyond the circle of believers to include all persons (neighbors)? Explain.

59

HOLINESS AND HOSPITALITY. 13:2

3. According to verse 2, what are we not to forget? In what way does the writer in verse 2a emphasize the importance of hospitality?

A woman long known for her hospitality has a plaque hanging on a wall in her home which reads, "Come in the evening, or come in the morning, come when you're looked for or come without warning."

4. In what way does hospitality reflect Christ's love to others? Why is it sometimes easy or tempting to "forget" to be hospitable?

5. List excuses some persons give for not being hospitable? Which if any are valid? Why? Which ones are not valid? Why?

6. Define "hospitality." Based on your definition think about how "hospitable" you have been over the past month. In what ways, if any, could you better fulfill the command in Hebrews 13:2?

HOLINESS AND SYMPATHY. 13:3

7. According to verse 3, what are we to do and from what perspective are we to do it?

8. Note use of the word "prison" in verse 3. Do you think the word should be interpreted to mean just those in criminal confinement or should the interpretation carry to other "prisons"? Explain. If interpreted in a broad sense, what could prison mean?

9. List examples of specific actions you could take to fulfill verse 3. Place a check mark beside those you are willing to follow up on.

10. What are some common "mistreatments" in our society of which you are aware? What can the church do to confront and change the things you have listed?

HOLINESS AND MARRIAGE. 13:4

11. Why do you think the writer included verse 4 since his audience was made up of believers who already knew that immorality and adultery were sin?
12. In what ways should a relationship with Christ help a marriage?

HOLINESS AND SECURITY. 13:5-6

Our system of commerce and government seems to breed discontent. Often, the emphasis is on the material which cannot satisfy. There is so much discontentment. However, a relationship with Christ can change one's perspective. Holiness helps one achieve contentment.

13. What are we to do (v. 5)? What promise does the believer have according to verse 5? How can focusing on the promises of verse 5 help you find contentment? What does "love" (v. 5) imply about the individual's priority? How can a "love" of money or constant lack of "contentment" destroy a person's spiritual life?
14. In what way is the Lord a "helper" (v. 6)? What is involved in receiving the help He offers?

HOLINESS AND LEADERSHIP. 13:7, 17-19

Only holiness of heart and life equips men and women for positions of leadership in the church. Learning, organizational ability, and a persuasive personality are all good — and can bring success — but they are not enough. From the days following Pentecost to the present, the first requirement for leadership is that the person be ". . . full of the Spirit and wisdom" (Acts 6:3). Only holiness will prevent the corruption of authority and the manipulation of people for self-gratification (I Peter 5:1-3). It is a joy to follow leaders who follow God, and it makes the task of caring for the flock easier for the shepherds.

15. What responsibilities are placed on both the believers who make up the body of believers and the persons who lead them (v. 7)? How are believers to obey their leaders and submit to their authority (v. 17)? What responsibility is implied

for leadership according to verse 17?
What affect does obedience have on
leadership?

16. What request is made in verse 18? Describe how you feel toward a leader who
sincerely makes such a request. Does
elevation to leadership lessen or increase
the need for honesty and prayer even in
personal problems? Explain.

HOLINESS AND STABILITY. 13:8-9

When the epistle to the Hebrews was written there was great
political, social, and religious agitation and controversy. Change was in
the air. The Jews were in a nationalistic fervor even though subjugated
to Rome. It was a dangerous time for the early Christians. They were
persecuted with equal bitterness by the ruling Pharisees in Jerusalem
and the Romans, who with iron hand governed the world and tolerated
no threat to their Caesar. The Hebrew believers stood friendless and
alone. They needed something stable to cling to. The unchanging
Christ was their only hope. We also live in troubled and dangerous
times. There are world leaders today who would stamp out Christianity. We fall back on holiness of heart and life to rest in faith in our
unchanging Christ. "The eternal God is our refuge, and underneath are
the everlasting arms . . ." (Deuteronomy 33:27). He has always been
thus. Thank God!

17. In what way is Jesus Christ unchanging
(v. 8)? How should the believers' life-
style be affected?

18. How does holiness provide stability for
daily living and prevent backsliding
(v. 9)?

HOLINESS AND THE ALTAR. 13:10-14

The Hebrew Christians were being denied the fellowship of the
Temple and synagogues. The Christian Jew had at last come to grips
with the reality that it was impossible to agree with his unconverted
countrymen. The Christians, the minority, were thrust out amid persecution and ridicule. Union or fellowship is the keynote of chapter 13
of Hebrews. From the opening exhortation, "Keep on loving each
other as brethren" (13:1) the writer goes on to press the claims of fellowship on behalf of strangers, those in prison, church leaders, and
others. All are called to one fellowship of worship at the altar which is
Christ on His cross.

19. What is the Christian's altar (v. 10)? Is it bound to any specific location? Are there Christian symbols which may serve to remind us of the altar? Explain.

20. How does Christ make us holy (v. 12)? What does verse 13 reveal about Christ's suffering? How can we recognize and resist temptations to compromise religious convictions, biblical truth, and that which would lead us away from holy living (vv. 13-14)?

21. In what way does verse 14 provide a basis for resisting that which would cause us to compromise our faith?

HOLINESS AND SACRIFICE. 13:15-16

22. How is it possible to ". . . continually offer to God a sacrifice of praise . . ." (v. 15)? What types of "sacrifices" are listed in verse 16? How can the Holy Spirit help us give such sacrifices?

HOLINESS AND EQUIPMENT. 13:20-25

The writer's closing benediction highlights the power of God's equipping — holiness of heart. He stresses in a few final statements the power and practicality of a faith founded on the power of the Spirit working in and through us.

23. List the foundation truths of Christian doctrine contained in verses 20-21. How are verses 20-21 an overview of the Bible from Genesis to Revelation?

24. What do verses 22-25 reveal to you about the writer's relationship and concern for his readers?

INSIGHT/ACTION

25. Throughout this study of Hebrews the theme "the better way" has often resurfaced in a variety of ways. Based on your study of Hebrews, describe in a brief paragraph why life in and through the Holy Spirit is "the better way."

26. Use Bible commentaries and concordances to study what is meant by "holiness" or "Christian perfection." List in your study diary specific references to verses found in Hebrews and what you think is meant by the terms in each instance.

27. Select and memorize from Hebrews 13 verses that are very meaningful to you.